CompTIA A+

Complete Study Guide

220-901 Exam

By

Moaml Mohmmd

&

By Max Beerbohm

1st Edition

3

Chapter VIII

Introduction

What is CompTIA Certification?

CompTIA (Computing Technology Industry Association) certification can be described in many ways, but the best way is to say it's a major certification for anyone working in the computer and information technology (IT) industry. CompTIA is the world's leading tech association, and the many types of certifications they offer all meet the industry standards. Here is an overview of the CompTIA certification and the benefits of obtaining CompTIA certifications.

What are CompTIA Certifications?

When we hear the words CompTIA certification, we often think of various computer-related certifications because CompTIA offers various certifications. However, the basic CompTIA certification is A+ (A Plus). The CompTIA A+ is an entry-level certification generally earned by computer service technicians. To obtain the A+ certification, an individual must pass an exam that demonstrates the individual's knowledge and skill in operating, installing, customizing and maintaining computers.

The A+ exam, which is aimed at individuals with at least six months of computer service technician experience, contains up to 90 multiple-choice questions and must be completed in 90 minutes. Once earned, the CompTIA A+ certification is good for three years. To maintain A+ certification, the individual must complete continuing education credits or retake the exam. U.S. News & World Report recommends taking the A+ exam as part of the required education to work as a computer support specialist.

Other Types of CompTIA Certifications

CompTIA offers various other certifications in addition to the A+.

These are for the basic knowledge of computers and are considered as core exams.

CompTIA IT Fundamentals

CompTIA Network+

CompTIA Security+

These are advanced certification exams and are more for individuals who are focused on infrastructure.

CompTIA Cloud+

CompTIA Linux+

CompTIA Server+

These three are focused on security.

CompTIA CySA+

CompTIA SASP

CompTIA PenTest+

These three are professional-based certifications.

CompTIA Project+

CompTIA CIT+

CompTIA Cloud Essentials

Why Obtain Certification?

Any time an employee works at a job that may involve some sort of certification, the employee should consider obtaining that certification. Certifications are especially important for a couple of reasons. CompTIA certifications are a way for the IT professional to demonstrate his or her knowledge of computers or specific areas of computers. Computers are utilized in almost all industries and jobs today, so it's important that the employee show that he or she is as knowledgeable as possible in computers.

When pursuing a certain job in the IT field, applicants who have CompTIA certifications listed on the resume will typically have the advantage. CompTIA is the leader in the computer and IT industries. CompTIA indicates that the IT sector is set to have another strong year in 2019, so those pursuing these careers should obtain as many CompTIA certifications as possible for the best job opportunities.

***

CompTIA is a nonprofit commercial organization specializing in the field of computer and information technology IT and is the largest provider of specialized certificates in this field. It is headquartered in the United States, and its certificates are spread across more than 120 countries, offering annually over 50 subjects to keep abreast of the most important developments in the field of computer and IT.

The certificates provided by the organization are divided into several levels, some of which are directed to beginners as an IT Fumdamentals certificate, and among them are directed to professionals such as A +, Cloud +, Network +, Project +, Server +, etc., and there are specialized certificates such as CDIA +, Cloud Essentials, and others, and advanced level certificates as a certificate CASP. These certificates are distinguished by not being biased towards a specific company, product or operating system, and we find that the largest companies associated with computers and related matters are members of this organization, including Microsoft, AMD, and thousands of others.

What is an A + Certificate?

The A + certification is the first step towards a professional IT support profession, although the "IT Fumdamentales" certification takes precedence over it. A + certification proves its owner's ability to understand hardware and operating systems and software applications and solve their problems, and also proves his competence by dealing with complex matters arising from various technical devices on the job site. After obtaining it, you can continue in the field of computer architecture, the field of operating systems, or the field of network administration, and obtain the following certificate that suits the field you prefer, and also help increase your employment opportunity in major technical companies, including someone who sets the A + certificate as a criterion for accepting the job Or ask the staff to get it. It is a neutral certification as it includes various technologies and operating systems.

What are the subjects covered in the certificate?

Those who want to obtain an A + certification must pass two exams to obtain them, which are CompTIA A + 220-901 and CompTIA A + 220-902. The first or second exams can be started, but it is preferred to start the exam 220-901 first.

Exam 220-901

This exam highlights understanding Terminology terms related to hardware and computer and performing basic hardware related tasks such as upgrading computer RAM, network basics, support for mobile devices, and troubleshooting. The main topics include the following chapters:

1. Hardware:

Characteristics of the motherboard components and their respective functions.

Configuring BIOS settings BISO / UEFI.

Balancing different types of memory and knowing their characteristics.

Install all types of expansion cards, storage devices, peripherals, etc. And adjust their settings.

Installing various types of processors on the computer and choosing the appropriate cooling system.

Choose and connect the appropriate feeder.

Balancing the different types of printers, knowing handling and maintaining them.

2. Networking:

Network cable specifications and connections.

Understanding TCP / IP and knowing the most important ports used.

Wireless networks, and devices used in network architecture.

3. Mobile Devices:

Installing the laptop hardware and adjusting all its settings.

Characteristics and advantages of various mobile devices.

Balancing portable ports.

4. Troubleshooting: Includes all previous hardware errors and problems and how to find solutions to them.

The following table shows the percentage of each department's contribution to the exam.

Domain	Percentage of Examination
1.0 Hardware	34%
2.0 Networking	21%
3.0 Mobile Devices	17%
4.0 Hardware & Network Troubleshooting	28%
Total	100%

Exam 220-902

This exam builds on the previous exam and its sections revolve around dealing with and installing various operating systems and setting their settings, security and protection measures, and troubleshooting. Its main topics include:

1. Windows operating system:

Balancing the features and requirements of Windows operating systems from Windows Vista to Windows 8.1 and installing them on a computer.

Use the Windows command line, control panel and other tools.

Adjust network settings.

Use Windows tools for preventive maintenance.

2. Other operating systems and technologies:

Learn about the most important functions and tools of macOS and Linux.

Virtualization.

Basics of cloud computing.

Network Hosts Services.

Mobile operating systems.

3. Security:

Learn about most protection threats.

Protection measures applied.

Protect mobile devices.

4. Troubleshooting:

Problems and crashes include the aforementioned operating systems and how to solve them.

5. Operational Procedures: This includes how to use and implement security and safety procedures, technical communication with others, and others.

The following table shows the contribution rate of the main subjects to the exam.

Domain	Percentage of Examination
1.0 Windows Operating Systems	29%
2.0 Other Operating Systems & Technologies	12%
3.0 Security	22%
4.0 Software Troubleshooting	24%
5.0 Operational Procedures	13%
Total	100%

Mechanism for taking the exam

The candidate must prepare well before taking the exam, so the organization provides a set of tools and e-books and exam samples to prepare for the self and get them when purchasing the exam by paying an additional amount, and it is recommended that the candidate obtain experience of not less than six months in the same field before applying for the exam. The next step is to pay the examination fee and reserve a place to take it through the Pearson VUE exam provider, where you choose the country and the approved examination center and book an appointment for you. The cost is $ 205 per test, that is, the certification cost is $ 410, and may vary by geographic region. The test is available in several languages, including English, German, Japanese and Spanish.

Obtaining the certificate and its validity

You must pass the two exams to obtain the certification, the passing score of 220 -901 is 675 out of 900 and the passing score of 220 -902 is 700 from 900. The number of questions is 90 questions and the test duration is 90 minutes, and questions are of multiple choice type and fill in the blanks.

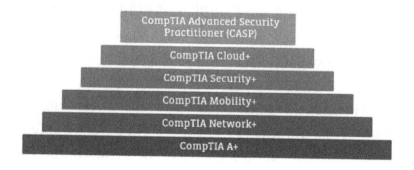

A + certificate is valid for a period of three years starting from the date of its attainment and there are several options for its renewal, including obtaining another certificate from CompTIA with a higher level as shown in the picture or others provided that you are related to the field of information technology as its history extends until the date of expiry of the certificate that got Accordingly, it is possible to renew the certificate by participating in some Continuing Education (CE) Activities to collect a number of points that qualify you to renew your degree, and to select the most appropriate option for you to browse the contents of this page well.

If you see that this certificate is what you are looking for, you can complete this series and start preparing for the first test to start your desired career.

Book on test 220-901

In this book, you will get acquainted with the most important topics mentioned in the test 220-201 and it is assumed that you are aware of some of the basics and types of computers and that your English is good, as the exam will be in the English language, and that you have a strong heart to decipher the computer and its components if the need arises to apply what you learn.

Chapter one
Motherboard

In this lesson, the first of a series of lessons on the CompTIA A + 220-901 exam, we will start with an explanation of the most important parts of a computer which is a motherboard and we will review how it works and its components with an explanation of the function of each.

Reboot

A personal computer consists of multiple elements that work together to perform a task such as calculation, writing, drawing, etc. It has certain characteristics and advantages, and most of these devices are removable and replaceable.

We will start with the most important of these components, which is the motherboard and also called the main board or the system board, which is a board with printed circuits on which its function is to connect all the computer components with each other via Buses and provide a suitable way to communicate between them to perform the tasks, and represents the backbone of the computer. The motherboard is characterized by a Form factor that determines its dimensions and its component elements.

Form factor

The motherboard is a Printed Circuit Board made of Fiberglass and copper and may be seen by one panel but it is made up of multiple layers, four layers or more, depending on the manufacturer, the quality and the components that make up the plate, and the size of the plate and the way its elements are positioned is determined by a factor called "factor" Shape "The most popular form factor used is Intel designed by ATX

Note the dimensions and the difference in the distribution of elements and their number in the image:

Pico-ITX

Nano-ITX

Mini-ITX

Micro-ATX

Standard-ATX

Motherboard components

The motherboard contains many elements:

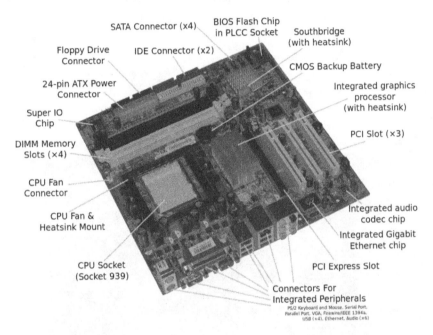

SATA Connector (x4)

BIOS Flash Chip
in PLCC Socket

Southbridge
(with heatsink)

Floppy Drive
Connector

IDE Connector (x2)

24-pin ATX Power
Connector

CMOS Backup Battery

Super IO
Chip

Integrated graphics
processor
(with heatsink)

DIMM Memory
Slots (×4)

PCI Slot (×3)

CPU Fan
Connector

CPU Fan &
Heatsink Mount

Integrated audio
codec chip

Integrated Gigabit
Ethernet chip

CPU Socket
(Socket 939)

PCI Express Slot

Connectors For
Integrated Peripherals
PS/2 Keyboard and Mouse, Serial Port,
Parallel Port, VGA, Firewire/IEEE 1394a,
USB (x4), Ethernet, Audio (x6)

CPU Socket

This socket provides a physical and electronic connection between the motherboard and the processor, and each processor has a dedicated socket and two or more processors may share one socket. The second is for PGA (Pin Grid Array) processors, and we will explain it later in the processors lesson, and the name of the socket is written on the board next to it or directly on it.

Buses

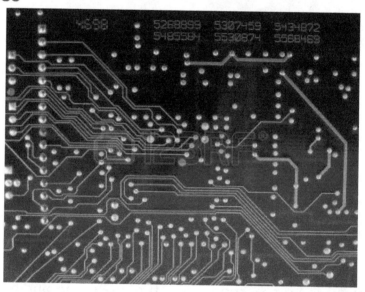

  They are copper wires printed on the motherboard and function for data transmission and electrical current. The carrier is characterized by a bit width and a speed measured in MHz. The vectors you see above and below the board are for the first and last layer of the panel.

Northbridge and Southbridge

They are of Integrated Circuit type and are integrated on the motherboard, and the North Bridge - also called Chipset - is larger than the South Bridge and closer to the processor, and is similar to the administrator of the Office of the Director-General, no one only communicates with him through him. The function of the north bridge is to connect all elements of the motherboard with the processor via the Front-Side Bus (FSB), where the memory and screen card (separate from the motherboard) and the south bridge connect with the processor, while the rest of the elements connect to the south bridge, including the audio chip, USB ports and ports SATA / IDE, expansion slots, etc. This is illustrated in the following figure.

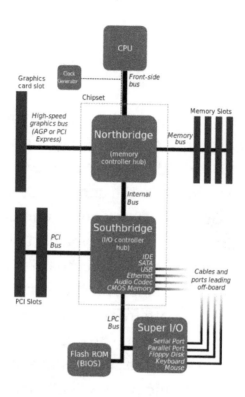

Is your display card integrated or separate ?! We often ask this question especially if we want to buy a computer for drawing and engineering design, if the display card is integrated, it is within the north bridge, that is, integrated with it on the motherboard, and then its efficiency and memory are less, but if it is separate, it is installed on its own slot and we will mention it later.

The north bridge determines the capacity and type of memory as it is controlled via a "Memory Controller Chip"

(MMC) located within it via a bus called "Memory Bus" and it consists of three parts, one of which is to control the memory and the second to send addresses and the third to send data data and it is shown in the picture .

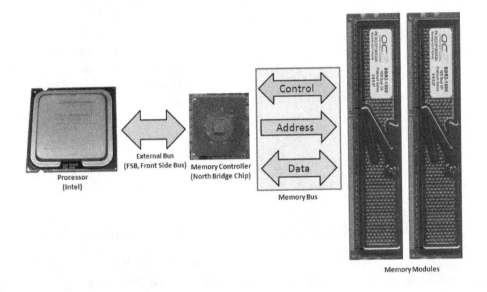

There is a bus between the north bridge and the processor called "Address Bus", in addition to the front bus, its function is to transfer the addresses of files that the processor requests from memory to process, as the processor sends the address of the file stored in memory to the memory controller, which in turn sends it via the address bus to memory, The memory then sends the file via the data bus to the north bridge and from it to the processor via the front bus to process this file and then returns to the memory in the same way. If you get lost between vectors, all you have to do is look at the image and quietly read the previous text.

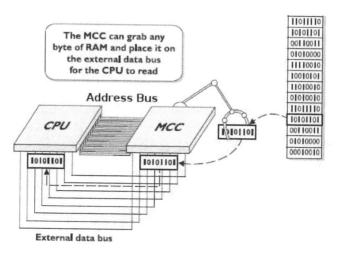

The MCC can grab any byte of RAM and place it on the external data bus for the CPU to read

Address Bus

CPU

MCC

External data bus

If the width of the address bus between the north bridge and the processor is 32 bits, the largest amount of memory you can connect to your computer is 4 GB because 232 = 4 GB. The higher the width of the bus, the greater the amount of memory that can be connected. Did you know now why they are telling you if you have 4 GB or more installed 64-bit operating system?

The north bridge also determines the type and speed of the processor, as the front carrier is at a certain speed, so for example, 200 MHz, the processor speed is 3200 MHz resulting from multiplying by 16 by the number 200, and the number 16 is called the Multiplier multiplication factor. If the north bridge does not support the bus speed of 200 or does not support the multiplication factor 16, you will not get a processor speed of 3200 MHz, so pay careful attention to the compatibility of the processor with the north bridge.

Sometimes the north bridge is combined with the south bridge in one circuit, so don't be surprised if you find no traces of the south bridge in some panels. The north bridge is provided with a heat sink or a fan for the intense heat emitted from it, while sometimes the south bridge is provided with a small heat sink above it. Because the north bridge is so important, you will find sellers calling the motherboard the name of its northern bridge.

Memory slots

They are dedicated memory ports and are located to the right of the processor and are characterized by the presence of two locks on both sides and support one type of memory (DDR2 or DDR3 ... etc.) and the number varies according to the motherboard structure and performance and form factor and ranges from 1 to 4 in the regular motherboard. And you should pay attention to the presence of a furrow in this part during the installation of the memory and if you do not install the memory on it make sure the compatibility between them.

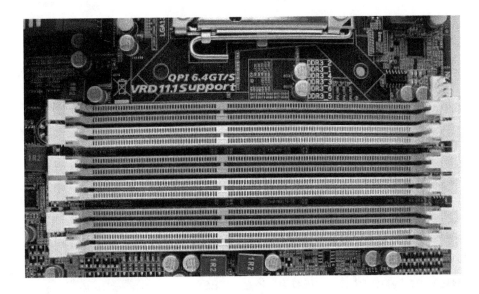

Expansion Slots

Used to connect additional devices to the motherboard, it expands its work, and these devices include the display card, modem card, sound, etc. It is located in the southern part of the plaque and has several types:

- **ISA**: It is a very old slit that is large in size and brown in color and is no longer used because it is slow and replaced by the type PCI.

- **PCI**: Created by Intel in 1993 and spread very quickly due to its speed and great development and used until these days, this slot works 32-bit or 64-bit width at a frequency of 33 MHz and reaches 133 MHz in the motherboard Servers. There is a PCI-X which is several times faster than the PCI type and there is a newer version of it, PCI-X 2.0.

- APG: The display card was installed on PCI slots connected with the south bridge and from it to the north, then the processor, which gives limited performance. This notch connects directly to the north bridge, and there is a newer type of it called AGP express.

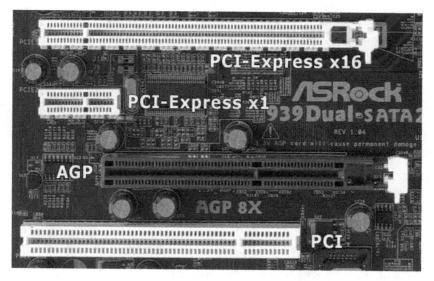

- PCI-e: Developed by Intel in 2004 and faster than PCI and AGP. With the advent of two types, the previous two types began to become extinct, as they are used with display cards, modems, network ... etc. It has many types, namely PCI-e (X1-X4-X8-X16), and often uses the type PCI-e

X16 with display cards, and it features a lock at the end, and the image shows the difference between them in form and performance.

-CNR, AMR, and ACR slots: Slots designed for a specific type of card such as network card, modem, and voice, characterized by brown color and small size and not intended for the average user.

Note: If you do not know the type of fissure, look for its name and type around it. It is printed on the plate and may be written in small print, or you may not see it as a result of dust accumulation.

Feed ports

These ports are used to supply the motherboard with the energy necessary for its operation. There are three types:

- **ATX port**: is the main port for feeding the motherboard with power via the cable coming from the Power Suplay feeder. Either the number of holes is 20 or 24, depending on the amount of power needed by the motherboard.

-**ATX 12 volt**: This port is located next to the processor and provides it with nutrition and consists of four holes.

- **Additional feeding ports**: Large performance motherboards or that contain a lot of expansion slots require more power, so additional ports have been added for this purpose, including the EPS 12 volt port, which powers the motherboard that contains more than one processor.

6-8 pin EPS +12 volt power cable

PATA / IDE port

Primary IDE concetor
Secondary IDE connector

This port is named IDE or PATA Relative to Advanced Technology Attachment (ATA) in Parallel Parallel, and this port connects the hard disk and drive to the motherboard. The number of ports on the board is 2, one of which is primary, white, and the other, Scondary, blue. Each port connects up to two devices as a maximum, that is, it can connect only 4 devices (hard disks or drivers). It is a very old and slow port and started to become extinct after the SATA port appeared.

SATA port

This port is based on the same technology as ATA, but the Serial transfer method is very different from the PATA port, so it is much faster than it. It is very fast, supports a cable length of up to 2 meters, and an external device can be connected to the board as an eSATA hard drive.

USB port

This port is used to connect external USB ports, such as the ones on the box from the front, and next to this port is written "USB" to distinguish it from the port of operating buttons in the Case box. The cable that we connect to this port is one piece and pay close attention to the correct direction while it is connected.

Connecting ports to the box body

It is located near the USB and SATA ports and used to connect the front buttons (play and restart, the operating light and the hard disk light) to the motherboard and next to it is written "F_PANEL", and the cables coming from the box may be scattered and individually and need a scheme to connect them shown in the following picture, and they may be one piece Similar to USB connection cable and connecting it then very easy. The Speaker port is located next to the previous port and is responsible for the sound you hear while the computer is running.

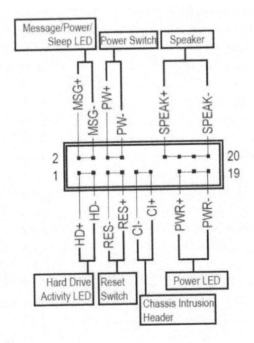

Conclusion

In this lesson, you learned the functionality of the motherboard and some of its components in theory. However, after completing reading these words, I advise you to go directly to your desktop computer and open the box cover to know practically the motherboard and its components. We will complete the rest of the elements in the next lesson.

Photo rights

Picture of North and South Bridge, published by Creative Commons BY-SA license, Moxfyre owner.

We'll complete the rest of the items and ports on the motherboard, which are:

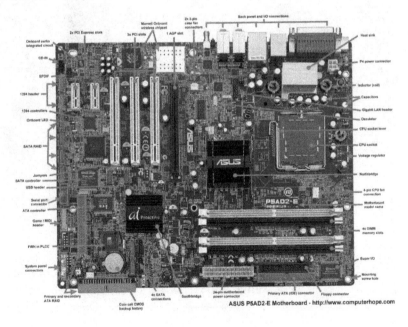

ASUS P5AD2-E Motherboard - http://www.computerhope.com

BIOS

The term BIOS (Basic Input / Output System) refers to the basic system of input and output, which is of the type "Firmware", which is a program that controls the hardware and is located on an electronic chip and its function is to configure and equip the hardware during the process of booting the computer Booting, which is the first program that works at startup.

(Pius 686 from American Megatrends. Published by Creative Commons BY-SA license via Wikimedia to its owner Raimond Spekking)

The BIOS is divided into two parts, the first is ROM (Read Only Memory), i.e., non-adjustable, on which the program is stored, and the other section is a SRAM type called CMOS (complementary metal-oxide-semiconductor) that stores the adjustments we make while adjusting BIOS settings, CMOS memory requires a current to keep these settings, so there is a small battery on the motherboard that supplies this memory and is called a CR2032 type CMOS battery. The main manufacturers of BIOS, American Megatrends and Phoenix are the BIOS.

Takeoff process

The main task of BIOS is to start the computer boot and equip the hardware through a process called POST (Power-On Self-Test) that examines all the hardware of the computer and identifies it and prepares it to work as a processor, memory, display card, keyboard ... etc. Then the Boot Loader takes over to start the first operating system that he finds on storage devices such as the hard disk, if there is no error or malfunction in one of the basic components of the computer's work, and if there is an error, something is sent with a symbol to be displayed on the screen if possible and alerts are issued Also sound with this error (for each sound alert error) via the speaker connected to the motherboard and the boot process stops, the benefit of the sound and the symbol is to know the fault directly and its repair and each BIOS manufacturer has its own error codes.

The boot process can be controlled by choosing a specific device to boot from after the POST process has been completed safely via the "Boot priority" option from BIOS settings or by pressing a specific button (the name of the button appears at the bottom of the screen for a short time when running) such as F12 or ESC when the computer is turned on to select the device You want to boot from, such as a laser drive, removable devices (flash drives), or over the network.

BIOS settings

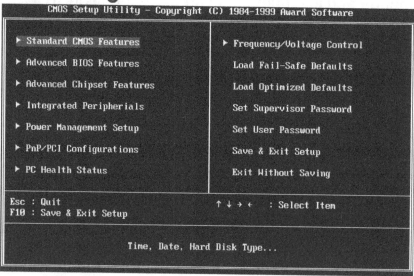

(Photo credit for Award Software International Inc)

You can enter BIOS settings by pressing the DEL button, for example, or a group of buttons, including ALT + CTRL + DEL. The name of this button will appear for a short time while taking off at the bottom of the screen, such as "Press F1 to enter CMOS setup". These settings include the following:

- Adjusting the settings of all gear components such as changing the operating mode or the frequency of one of the elements (the processor speed can be broken by increasing the frequency of the FSB front carrier or changing the multiplying factor).

Adjust the system clock.

Turning hardware components on or off (such as turning off some ports, such as the USB port or disabling the built-in sound card).

- Boot priority order (such as taking off from the laser driver first and then the hard drive second).

- Add passwords to protect BIOS settings from strangers and hackers by preventing them from tampering with them or changing the boot process to enter and hack your computer, and also to protect the hard drive with a password to prevent access to files if they are stolen.

- Control the operating fans connected to the motherboard as an increase or decrease the speed.

Reprogramming

In modern computers, the BIOS can be reprogrammed by scanning its content and then writing new content. This process is called "Flashing" and we use it to improve performance by updating the current version or to support new devices that are not supported by the current version (if the incompatibility between the new component and the motherboard) or if a program is corrupted The BIOS.

The type of memory most recently used is EEPROM, i.e. the memory can be scanned and programmed electronically using operating system software provided by the manufacturer, such as @BIOS motherboard or Gigabyte.

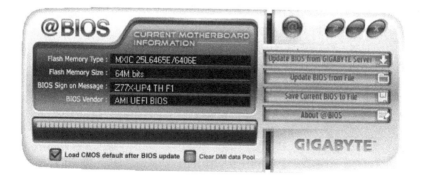

BIOS can also be programmed via its settings from the Flash BIOS option. ASUS provides this feature with its motherboards called "EZ Flash" and finds them in advanced settings. To work this way, you must download the BIOS version of your motherboard from the manufacturer's website and place it on a flash drive, for example, then enter This tool (Flash BIOS) and locate the file to update the BIOS version.

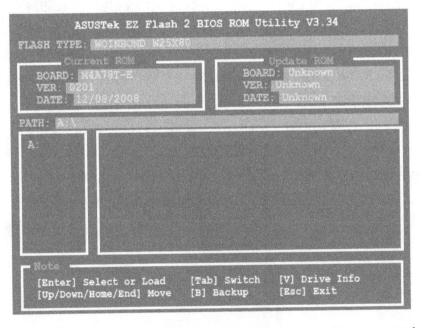

Note: the BIOS may be EPROM memory, and this cannot be programmed electronically, but via a device that is often used by electronics engineers and they call it "programmed". This type is rarely used and is likely to be encountered in your working life.

The UEFI system is a replacement for BIOS

The BIOS system retreated in the beginning of 2011 in favor of a new system called UEFI (Unified Extensible Firmware Interface), which was developed by Intel in 2005 where it was called then EFI, which is more complex than BIOS and is characterized by that it supports a larger hard disk capacity of more than 2.2 terabytes and up to 9.4 zettabytes, equal to 1024x1024x1024 GB, supports GPT Partition Table, which is a method of structuring and partitioning a hard drive instead of an MBR (Master Boot Record) that does not allow partitioning more than 4 main partitions. Also boot up speed, graphical interface, great security and support for many boot devices, as it also includes a shell UEFI Shell provides a command line to access many services by typing commands in it.

ITE chip and Winbond chip

They are two of the most popular types of integrated circuits that control the Input and Output units called the super I / O controller.

Designed in 1980, the super I / O function was ISA expansion and when not in use it was developed to include slow hardware control such as the Floppy disk and the

Parallel port - used with printers - and the mouse and keyboard that connects to the PS / 2 port. Some chips measure the temperature and control the speed of the fans that are connected to the motherboard, such as the processor fan and other functions. These circuits belong to two different companies and there are other companies including Nuvoton.

Integrated chips

There are a number of built-in cards on the motherboard, including the sound card, note its chip in the top left of the board where "Audio Integrated circuit" is written, and the Ethernet wired network card are often from Realtek and are the most famous in this field and find the company logo on the circuit.

Sometimes there is a wireless card as shown in the picture above. These circuits are located near their rear port (audio, network, etc.).

Back ports

They are ports for connecting some components, including the mouse and keyboard via the PS / 2 port, audio cables, USB devices, LAN cable, printer (legacy), external hard drives via the eSATA port, screen cable (if the display card is integrated), and others. Each chip port has an onboard IC controller.

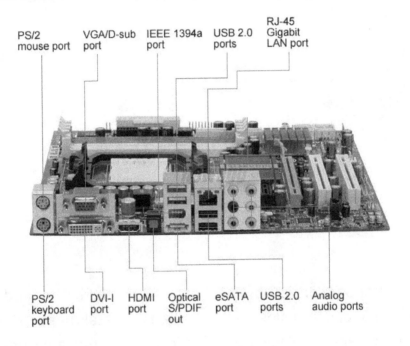

Electronic items

The motherboard contains a huge number of electronic elements such as resistors, capacitors, coils, transistors ... etc. Which controls the current and the voltage connected to its elements, and any defect with one of them may stop the plate from working or in the simplest case one of the elements may be damaged and stop working without affecting the entire board.

A file with an iron heart and a file with a ferrite heart

Capacitors

Jumper

The hopper consists of lined legs next to each other and a piece of plastic inside which contains a metal that carries the current. By placing the plastic piece on two adjacent legs, we allow the current to pass through it and close this circuit, the plate as a whole or one of its elements understands the flow of current in that circuit that it must activate some settings and cancel another.

Computer Jumper

Open   1-2 Jumped   2-3 Jumped

http://www.computerhope.com

See the example in the picture, the jumper is white and by placing it on the first and second legs we activate the "Normal" mode and by placing it on the second and third legs we activate the "Config" mode and removing it the status is "Recovery" so by using the jumper we managed to control three options. Be aware that settings differ from one hopped to another and from one panel to another.

Pop-up is found on some motherboards next to the CMOS battery, which is intended to reset BIOS default settings.

How to choose the right motherboard

If you want to buy and assemble a new desktop computer, you must choose the hardware and components for that computer, and I advise you to choose the motherboard first, then buy the rest of the hardware, depending on the board you chose. To buy the motherboard, first determine the main goal of buying a computer (is it to surf the Internet only, or for drawing or engineering design, or for games, etc.), and then pay attention to some things, including:

- The type of the north bridge chip, which determines the type and speed of the processor, the type of memory and its maximum capacity.

Form Factor (the size of the computer case depends on it).

Front FSB Frequency.

- The number and type of cracks used for the display card.

Number of expansion slits.

- The manufacturer (Intel, Gegabyte, ASUS, etc.) that determines the board's build quality and component quality, as this affects the overall computer performance and future malfunction rate.

The possibility to upgrade the board and update it in the future (such as paying attention to the types of processors supported by the processor socket).

- Integrated cards with the board (such as buying a board with a built-in wireless network card for a company's computers to provide the purchase of additional separate network cards).

Pay close attention to the compatibility between the motherboard, memory and processor to get the best performance and thus invest the full price you paid.

Conclusion

We terminated the motherboard issue and it is now assumed that the main elements should be identified by looking at any motherboard and specifying the function of those elements and the tasks associated with them.

Chapter II
CPU

The most important component of a computer is the Processor, called the Central Processing Unit, or the Microprocessor. Without it, there is no computer. It is an electronic circuit that executes instructions and processes data using calculations and logic.

The design and shape of the processor has changed a lot over recent decades, but its core work has remained constant. Modern processors these days are microprocessors, meaning that all components and elements of the processor exist in one integrated IC circuit, and this circuit may contain additional elements such as memory, microcontrollers, and others.

The processor is made of electronic components called semiconductors, which are transistors that contain millions of them. The advantages that transistors add to the processor are precision, lower energy consumption, and high speed.

Processor components

The processor consists of several components, the most important of which are:

Control Unit

It is a digital circuit that controls directing all commands and data to process it. It does not execute or process data, but rather addresses the memory, the unit of calculation, logic, and input and output devices and coordinates among them to implement the orders, so we find that the console manages and organizes most computers It also controls the amount of data traveling between the processor and all elements and devices, the flow of data inside the processor, and the organization of work of other units inside it.

ALU (Arithmetic Logic Unit)

It is a digital circuit responsible for the implementation and processing of data by performing arithmetic and logical operations. The calculation used is collection only. The rest of the operations can be rewarded and converted to the collection process.

Data comes from memory to the processor for processing within this unit and then returned to memory or stored temporarily in the registers which is very fast memory.

MMC (**Memory Management Unit**)

Expensive processors contain the memory controller whose function is to convert logical addresses into physical RAM addresses, secure memory protection, transfer data to a secondary storage device (such as a hard disk) and bring it from it, and it is of great use when using virtual memory. Simple or desktop processors may not have this unit.

Form factor

The Form factor describes the shape of the external processor and the type of socket it is installed on. The most popular form factors are:

LGA

It is a processor and circuit packing technology called LGA (Land Grid Array), where the bottom of the processor is provided with a network of small contacts that connect with the motherboard, and this type is installed on the socket or welded directly on the board. Among the processors that use this factor are "Intel Pentium 4", "Intel Xeon", "Intel Core 2", "Intel Core" and "AMD Opteron" as it is used by modern Intel processors unlike AMD processors that use PGA design frequently.

The most popular sockets that support the LGA form factor are the "LGA 775" socket, which is used by all "Intel Pentium D" and "Core 2" processors, and "LGA 1150", and the number 775 and 1150 indicate the number of legs on the socket.

PGA

It is a technique for packing the processor and circuitry and it is called PGA (Pin Grid Array) and the shape of the processor is square or rectangular and the legs are distributed under the processor regularly and does not cover the entire area, and this type is installed on the board through holes on it or via a socket, and it has many types:

- FC-PGA (Flip-Chip PGA): Intel designed this type with "Pentium III", "Celeron" and "Pentium 4" processors that use plugs:

Socket 370

Socket 478

- SPGA (Staggered PGA): used with Intel processors and the sockets that support it:

Socket 5

Socket 7

Socket 8

-CPGA (Ceramic PGA): This circuit is widely used by ICs, and some of the processors it uses are "AMD Athlon" and "AMD Buron" processors and plugs are:

Socket A

Socket AM2

Socket AM2 +

- **OPGA (Organic PGA):** used with integrated circuits and processors, and was originally invented by AMD company with "Athlon XP" processor, and the sockets used are:

Socket A

Socket 754

Socket 939

Socket 940

Socket FM1

Socket FM2

Socket AM2

Socket AM2 +

Socket AM3

Socket AM3 +

Socket AM4...

This technology is called Single Edge Contact Cartridge, also known as Slot 1, and has been used with the "Intel Pentium II" processor and the "Intel Pentium III" processor.

Cache memory

It is a very small and fast SRAM type memory located inside the processor or on the motherboard. It is used to reduce the time and energy needed to access data in the main memory (RAM), as it is used for storing frequently used data instead of returning it to memory and then bringing it back. The processor speed is very high compared to the main memory, so there will be a lot of waste in the time needed to transfer the information in the memory to the processor in the absence of cache.

The processors contain several types of this memory, such as cache memory for instructions and others for data that is divided into several levels.

Types of cache memory

Modern computers and servers contain three types of cache:

Instruction cache: increases the speed of retrieval and implementation of instructions.

Data cache: Increases the speed of obtaining data from the main memory or writing data on it to return it to the main memory, and is divided into levels which are:

-Level 1 L1: is a very fast memory with a small storage capacity (8 - 128 KB) integrated with the processor, and each core has a separate L1 memory core.

- The second level L2: is slower than the L1, but its capacity is greater (64 KB - 16 MB) and is combined with the processor. Each core may have a separate memory or all cores share the processor with one L2 memory.

-Level 3 L3: slower than its predecessor (its speed is a multiple of the main memory speed) and the largest capacity (4 - 128 MB) and almost all cores share one L3 memory.

- Level IV L4: rarely used, has a separate chip, and has capacity greater than 512MB.

TLB cache (translation Look-aside buffer): its function is to speed up the process of converting virtual addresses into physical addresses for instructions and data. There can be a separate instruction memory called ITLB (Instruction TLB) and a separate data memory also called DTLB (Data TLB), and this memory is part of the MMC memory controller.

Mechanism of working with the processor

The data to be processed moves between the main memory and cache as fixed cache blocks. When the processor wants to read from or write to the main memory, it first checks for a copy of the data in the cache. If the processor finds that data, it reads it directly from the cache memory and then stores the result in it. This process is much faster than reading from the main memory.

When the processor requests the data from the cache memory, it requests it first from the L1 memory. If it does not find it, it requests it from the L2 memory. If it does not find it, it searches it for the L3 memory. If it finds it, it takes it for processing, and if it does not find it, it is sent to the memory to bring that data.

If the processor does not find the data in the cache memory, this memory requests a copy of the data from the main memory, which in turn sends a copy of the data to it, and then the processor reads that data. After the completion of its processing, the data is sent to the cache memory, and then it is returned to the main memory; but if the processor needs that data again and again, it remains in it until the processor finishes it.

Multicore processors

A multi-core processor is a single processor that contains independent processing units, each called a "core". The multi-core processor can process many instructions at the same time, which increases its speed.

The nuclei may share a cache memory with each other, and each core may be unique to one or more levels of cache memory. The picture shows the structure of a dual-core processor in which each core has a unique L1 memory and the two cores share a L2 memory.

Some processors can simulate the work of two physical cores, called HT (Hyper Threading), which Intel developed on its processors. This means that if the quad-core processor supports this technique, it works as if it was an eight-core processor, and certainly this processor would not be equal to its counterpart which contains eight physical cores in performance.

Clock speed

This term refers to the frequency or frequency of the processor and is measured in Hz (number of pulses per second), that is, the number of instructions processed per second, and the processor speed is currently measured in GHz. For example, a processor with a speed of 1 hertz can handle one thing per second, and a processor with a speed of 3 gigahertz can handle 3 billion orders per second.

32-bit and 64-bit processor architecture

The processor architecture whether 32-bit or 64-bit affects its performance and determines the type of operating system and software used with it, but what is the difference between them? The difference between the 32-bit processor and 64-bit processor is:

Processing word size per pulse: The 32-bit processor can handle 32-bit data and the 64-bit processor handles 64-bit data in each pulse and therefore has an impact on the amount of data processed.

Address bus display: (We explained it in the motherboard lesson) as it determines the maximum memory that the processor can handle. 32-bit processors have a 32-bit address width and can handle 4 GB of memory as a maximum, while 64-bit processors have a 64-bit bus width The amount of memory you can handle is large.

Buy and install a processor on the motherboard

Before buying a new processor you must take into account all the previous matters and not focus on the speed only, and do not forget also compatibility with the motherboard (front carrier frequency FSB and multiplication factor and socket type) to invest the full price of the processor that you paid.

Be careful when installing the processor that there are some signs that help to install it, including the presence of an arrow in one of the corners of the processor, offset by an arrow similar to it on the socket or the presence of some protrusions on the socket that indicate the correct way to install the processor. And beware of using violence during the installation of the processor, especially with PGA type processors, any wrong movement leads to a broken leg and a processor or socket malfunction.

Install the appropriate cooling device on it after installing it on the socket, or the cooling system is a fan with a heat sink, and in this case do not forget to add a little cooling paste that improves the transfer of heat from the surface of the processor to the dispersion, liquid cooling or gas cooling.

Conclusion

In this chapter, we learned many things about the processor, which are just the tip of the iceberg, but it is sufficient to understand the principle of the processor, its components and specifications.

Chapter III

Hard disk: structuring, specification and configuration

In the previous lesson we talked about the types of memory and we covered in some detail the random memory and its types. In this lesson, we have two parts to talk about memory, but this time about secondary memory: the hard disk.

Reboot

After the invention of the computer, there was a need to have a memory that permanently keeps data without losing it, so the first hard disk appeared in 1956, which was invented by IBM to meet after developing this need.

A hard disk is a permanent storage device, and it relies on the magnetic principle of data storage. The hard drive is categorized as a mechanical device because it contains mobile mechanical elements for storing and reading data. The data is stored in the hard disk randomly, meaning that it can be written and read in any location of the disk without any sequence or arrangement.

The most important advantages of the hard drive that gained this fame are its large capacity, good performance and low price, as its storage capacity exceeds 2 terabytes, and the most famous hard disk manufacturers are Seagate, Toshiba and Western Digital.

Hard drive components

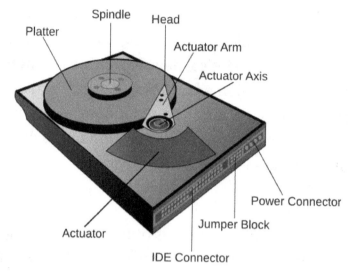

The hard drive contains four basic components:

Discs Platters

They are round discs made of aluminum, glass, or ceramic and coated with a layer of iron oxide or a mixture of magnetized metal for storing data on it, followed by a thin layer of carbon to protect from the damage caused by the reading reading heads.

Read / write heads

The reading and writing heads are located on the discs without touching their surface, and each disk has two reading and writing heads, one for the upper surface and one for the lower surface. These headers write and read data on the magnetic layer, and are loaded onto the arms that are driven by an electric motor.

Electric motors

The hard drive has two actuators, one for moving Actuator read and write heads and one for spindle drive on Spindle. As for the first, it moves the arm according to a circular arc along the radius of the disc. Thus, when the discs revolve, the heads cover the entire surface, and the second rotates the axis that holds all the discs according to a fixed number of rotations such as 7200 revolutions per minute (RPM). These motors are controlled by circuit boards.

Electronic board

It is a PCB printed circuit board on which circuits controlling motors and converting incoming and outgoing signals, electronic elements, and SRAM type cache (to store data in them while they are sent to the main memory or written to disks due to a wide difference in speeds), the data connection port and the connection port Powered.

Note: Any malfunctions that occur in this panel can be fixed as they are visible at the bottom of the hard disk, while the previous elements cannot be accessed because they are inside a vacuum chamber and any attempt to open the hard disk or remove the adhesive that prevents the entry of air loaded with dust particles into the room leads to disk damage Crucifixion, reading and writing heads are damaged, and the process of opening the room requires professionals in this field with specialized tools.

Hard drive specifications

The hard disk has several specifications that must be taken into consideration because it affects its performance, namely:

Data latency: The time needed to move read and write heads to the location of data on the disk.

Spin speed: is the rotational speed of the disks, measured in one revolutions per minute (RPM). This time is called a "response time", which is the time required to place the required sector under the reading and writing head, and the response time is 4.16 milliseconds for a hard disk whose number of cycles is 7200 .

Data transfer rate: It is the amount of data transferred to and from the hard disk at one time and is related to the number of tracks and sectors, sector size, rotational speed and access time.

Storage capacity.

Formatting the hard drive

The operating system and applications use the hard drive only after it is formatted, and this process is divided into three phases.

Low level configuration

This configuration is performed by the manufacturer and is called "physical configuration" or "low-level formatting." It addresses hardware and is the disk surface structure on which the disk controller chip relies on writing and reading data.

The disc consists of two upper and lower surfaces and the numbering of the disks starts from the number 1, while the faces are numbered starting from the number 0 and then 1 ... etc. The surface is divided according to the following:

- **Tracks**: are concentric circular paths within which data are stored, and each path has a number. The external path is its number 0, followed by 1, and increases inward.

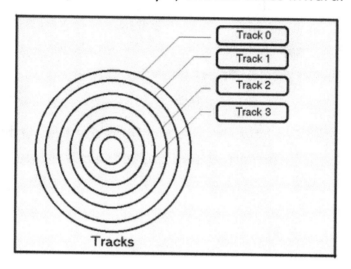

- **Cylinders**: The discs are placed on top of each other, so the tracks are on top of each other as well, and so we have what is called a "cylinder", which is all of the tracks located in the vertical plane passing through one of the paths. The file is stored on disk within the disk to reduce the movement of the read and write heads to and from other tracks, thereby increasing the speed of reading and writing.

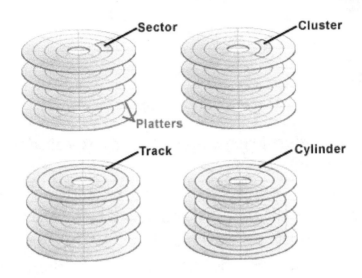

- **Sectors**: The path is divided into thousands of small parts called "sectors", which are the smallest hard disk storage units. Each sector has a fixed size, usually 512 bytes, and segment numbering begins at 1.

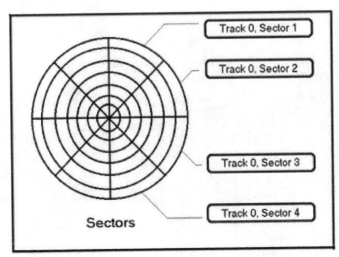

Clusters: Clusters join together to form a so-called "cluster" or "specialized unit" that is sized as the hard drive is formatted by the operating system. The storage of files is on the level of clusters, so if you have a text file with a size of 1 kilobytes and the cluster size is 2 kilobytes (4 sectors) then the file occupies the entire space of the cluster and remains 1 kilobytes without using and measure on that of the rest of the files, so you find when viewing the properties of the file two sizes one of them is the file size The original and other size it occupies on the hard drive. The smaller the cluster, the less waste the size of the hard disk, so it is best to reduce it if your files are small.

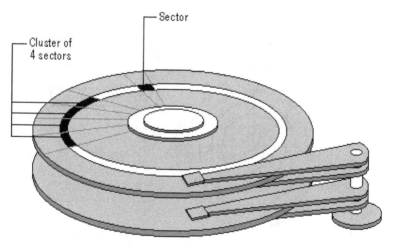

Retail Partitioning

Fragmentation is the division of all capacity of a hard disk into regions or parts called Partitions. The hard disk stores all information about these partitions as their location (beginning and end of the sector) and their size in a table called Partitions table and the operating system first reads it to show the partitions on that hard disk.

There are two hard disk partitioning and structuring systems and the MBR (Master Boot Record) fragmentation system that supports only four basic partitions or three primary partitions and extended partition, and does not support a capacity of more than 2 TB, which is old. The GPT fragmentation system (GUID Partition Table) that appeared in mid-2010 and is supported by most file systems today, is always preferred.

There are two main types of hashes:

Primary hash: This hash has only one file system in which the operating system and boot files are installed.

Extended fragmentation: a fragmentation that can be divided into subdivisions called "logical partitions". A hard disk can contain no more than an extended partition, but it can be used in conjunction with major partitions.

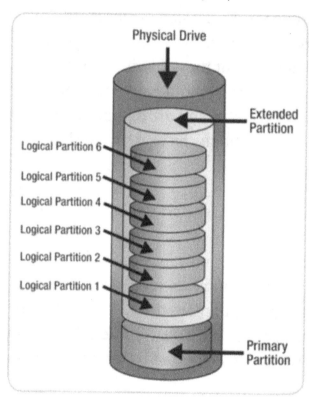

The new hard drive must be partitioned for use, and the operating system provides many programs for creating or modifying new partitions, such as resizing or deleting them.

Hard disk partitioning features include isolating the operating system and programs from personal files (operating system on fragmentation, personal files on fragmentation), installing multiple operating systems, isolating or protecting files. If fragmentation is damaged, files in other partitions remain intact, and increase the efficiency of the computer as a whole and others . One disadvantage is that it reduces hard disk performance because read and write heads have to switch back and forth between hashes to read files.

High-level configuration

In this type of format, the file system is created on hard disk partitions, which is used to control how storage, retrieval, management, and organization of files are partitioned. Each file system has a specific structure and logical rules that it uses to divide the file, put it on the disk and name it, then know its title and re-read it, and the file systems differ from each other with speed, flexibility, protection, size that support it and other characteristics.

Operating systems use multiple file systems such as NTFS and FAT32, which are supported by Windows, file systems from the ext family (ext2, ext3, and ext4), XFS and btrfs supported by Linux, and the HFS Plus file system supported by macOS.

Disk storage mechanism

The disk controller chip is responsible for translating the signals and moving the reading and writing head carriers to the location from which to read or write. The writing head changes the direction of the magnetization of the layer grains on the surface of the disk to represent the binary numbers (0 and 1) that are the Bits bits for writing on the disk, and the process of reading data is knowing the direction of the magnetization (polarity) at the site. The figure shows the reading and writing process.

Hard drive read/write head

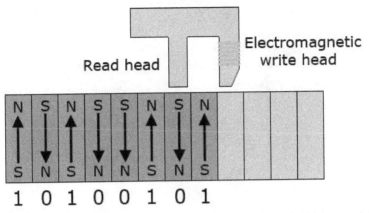

The problem of losing magnetization due to the excess heat arose because of the small size of the hard disk, as it is known that the heat negatively affects and dissipates the magnetization. To overcome this problem, companies resorted to multiple solutions, including adding a second layer of magnetic (iron oxide) parallel to the first layer and between them an insulating layer as this leads to its magnetization in the opposite direction to the upper layer, which supports and strengthens its magnetization.

Form factor

Have you ever seen the size of a laptop or desktop hard drive? Is there a difference between them?

Hard drive delivery techniques

The hard drive is connected to the motherboard via the data port and takes its feed from the power port that connects to the Power supply, and the forms of these ports vary according to the technologies supported by the hard disk. We will discuss the three most common techniques used:

PATA (Parallel ATA)

It is a technology for connecting storage devices such as hard disk and laser disk to computers and also called IDE. The data socket is 40 feet and the cable is 40 or 80 wires (the 80 wires are the fastest) and is of limited length, and the data transfer speed ranges from 16 to 133MB per second.

On the motherboard there are two PATA ports, one primary and one secondary (blue), and each cable supports two storage devices with the motherboard, i.e. the maximum number of devices is 4. When connecting two storage devices on the same cable, the jumper on these devices must be set to prioritize Boot, and there are three modes, Master and Slave and Automatic Capel select, where the "main" mode is specified for the device that contains the operating system to boot from and the "dependent" mode for the second device or leave the "automatic" mode for the two ready.

This technology is very old and slow, and has been replaced by a newer technology called SATA.

SATA technology (Serial ATA)

This technology is a development of the previous transfer technology and its advantages include reducing the cable size and cost (7 wires instead of 40 or 80), a large speed of data transmission (ranging from 150 to 1969 mbps), the number of ports is greater for connecting storage devices, and supports a cable length of two meters, It can connect storage devices without turning off the computer, and also supports connecting external storage devices via a technology called Esata.

There are versions of SATA technology that differ with speeds and some features, and they are SATA 1.0 or Serial ATA-150, as the number 150 indicates the data transfer rate in one megabyte per second, SATA 2.0 (Serial ATA-300) and even SATA 3.3, which was released in 2016 and has many advantages over Previous versions.

SAS (Serial Attached SCSI)

It is a technology for connecting storage devices as it supports the connection of 65535 devices which is faster than SATA and provides nutrition and data through one cable up to 10 meters in length. This technology is used in places where speed is very important, such as servers, and is rarely used in ordinary computers.

There are versions of this technology: SAS-1 with a speed of 375 Mbps, SAS-2 with a speed of 750 Mbps, SAS-3 with a speed of 1500 Mbps and the version of SAS-4 is currently under development.

SSD alternative

The hard disk has had some problems with its mechanical partition, especially when the temperature rises, which affects the magnetization of the discs and the problem of the expansion of the elements inside it. Meanwhile, digital memory has witnessed a major development of all kinds, which led to the disposal of the mechanical partition and the development of EEPROM memories instead of the SSD (Solid State Drive) as a new file storage device.

Chapter four
Feeder

The PSU (Power Supply Unit) is an electrical transformer that supplies all the components of a computer with energy. It is like fuel for cars, and the computer does not operate without it.

The power unit consists of multiple electronic elements (transformers, capacitors, transistors, resistors ... etc) whose function is to convert the AC (Alternating Current) of the city (220 or 110 volts) to DC (Direct Current) with the distribution of efforts to all computer elements and reducing them Compatible with each component.

The motherboard controls the shutdown and operation of the feeder, so when it sends a signal to the feeder to turn it on, it starts to self-check all its components and efforts. If there is no malfunction in the efforts or a malfunction in the elements, the feeder sends to the processor a signal called "PWR OK" or "PowerGood" informing it that the current is good and can start work, and in the event of a malfunction do not send that signal and then the processor does not give the command to start the operation And boot up and the computer does not work. A malfunction may occur at any moment, so a signal is sent directly to the processor to stop the computer from working, to avoid damaging any of its components.

Each feeder has three characteristics that play an important role in choosing the feeder: power, joint types, and form factor.

Power

It is the most important characteristics of the feeder, although the quality of manufacturing and the elements are also important, to determine the appropriate feeder for the computer.

Each component in the computer needs a certain amount of energy that collects all of its components, giving the value of the required power from the feed unit to work with good efficiency, so if the number produces 365 watts assuming then we choose a feed unit with greater capacity than it would be 400 or 500 watts, and if its capacity is less then it will not work Well it will crash. The following table shows the amount of energy for some computer components.

Device type	Power amount (watt)
AMD Athlon XP 1.5MHz-2.5GHz	66-77
AMD Athlon 64 3.0GHz-3.4GHz	89
Intel Pentium4 2.2GHz-2.4GHz	80-90
Intel Penyium4 2.4GHz-3.0GHz	90-105
ATX motherboard	40-65
DDR2 (PC2100)	10
CD-ROM drive	20
DVD-ROM drive	25
5400RPM IDE hard drive	15

7200RPM IDE hard drive	25
AGP video card	30-75
USB device	5
Fan	2

Instead of searching for all the computer components and manually calculating the power, some sites provide an easier way, such as the powersupplycalculator website and the bequiet website, to calculate the ability of the appropriate feeder for the computer to be assembled and purchased by specifying its specifications, and it suggests to you sometimes some of the types available in the market with its specifications and prices, preferably not less than the capacity 400 watts.

Types of connections

The feeder supplies power to the various components of the computer via cables of various voltage ends, with connections that fit the outlet of the element to be powered. Each link has a shape and number of legs that correspond to the port on which it is installed and it is impossible to install it on another port that does not suit it, so there is no room for error. The following table shows the types of links, their names, and their function.

Link shape	Name	Function
	20 pin ATX	Main board motherboard ATX 20-pin feed.
	20+4 pin ATX	Main board motherboard with ATX 20 or 24-man port.
	24 pin ATX	Main board motherboard with ATX 20 or 24-man port.

	4 pin ATX +12V	Feed the processor.
	8 pin EPS +12V	Feed two or more processors on the same board.
	4+4 pin +12V	Feed one or more processors.

	4 pin Molex	IDE-enabled peripherals, fans and more.
	SATA	SATA accessory feeding (Hard Disk and Driver).
	6 pin PCI Express	Additional PCIe expansion slots, port number 6.

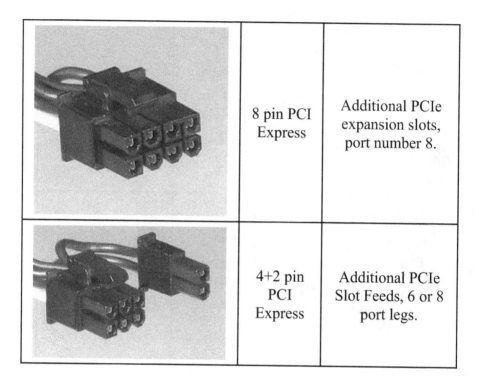

	8 pin PCI Express	Additional PCIe expansion slots, port number 8.
	4+2 pin PCI Express	Additional PCIe Slot Feeds, 6 or 8 port legs.

Form factor

Feeders are made according to a form factor that determines their size, shape, location of the cooling fan, and the types and connections of the joints. The choice of the form factor of the feeder depends on the size and shape of the box, the motherboard, and the direction the air is out of the fan as the fan contributes to drawing air from inside the computer box and throwing it out. The following table shows the most famous form factors.

Feeder shape	The motherboard form factor that supports it	Motherboard and processor feeder type	Form factor
	ATX, microATX, BTX, microBTX	20/24-pin, 4-pin +12V	ATX/ ATX12V
	microATX, FlexATX, microBTX, picoBTX, Mini-ITX, DTX	20/24-pin, 4-pin +12V	SFX/ PS3

	microATX, FlexATX, microBTX,p icoBTX, Mini-ITX, DTX	20/24-pin, 4-pin +12V	TF X1 2V

	microBTX, picoBTX, DTX	20/24-pin, 4-pin +12V	CF X1 2V
	microATX, FlexATX, microBTX, picoBTX, nanoBTX, Mini-ITX, DTX	24-pin, 4-pin +12V	Fle x AT X

Wire colors and functions

Have you noticed that each wire in the feeder cables is marked with a color? These colors indicate the value of the wire voltage and its function as the feed unit converts the frequency voltage into five continuous efforts that suit each component of the computer, and the colors of the wires with the value of their efforts and their function are:

Yellow: +12V

Blue: -12V

Red: +5V

White: -5V

Orange: +3.3 volts.

Violet: + 5V, used in "standby mode".

Black: grounding line.

Green: Used to power the feeder, and to connect it manually with the black wire. The feeder is on.

Gray: +5V, is used to ensure the integrity of the feeder.

Brown: Used to operate a computer remotely via a network card or modem.

The image below shows how to manually operate the feeder.

The feed module information is written on it, including effort, power, shape factor, etc. The following image shows a feed unit from spire with the form factor "ATX" and a maximum power value of 650 watts.

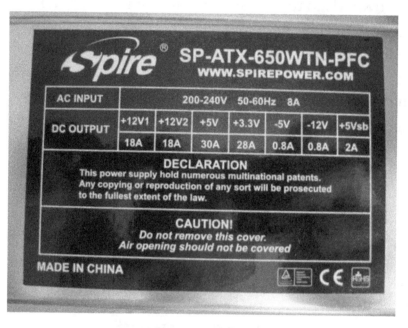

How to choose the right feed unit

The process of selecting a feeder is never random and you do not hear someone say "the bigger the better, the better" when determining capacity because you will often pay a surplus price for a feeder that you do not need. The appropriate form factor of the box, the type of connections and their number must be taken into consideration, depending on the type of motherboard.

Avoid purchasing cheap feed units because they are poor quality and poorly manufactured, which causes future malfunctions and damage to some components of the motherboard as a result of the change in the value of the efforts the greater the use and thus you may pay a higher cost than if you choose a high quality feed from the beginning.

Chapter V

Printers and their types

Printer is an electromechanical device that converts all electronic copies, whether they are books, electronic documents, pictures, plans ... etc. To hard copies. Typists are connected to the computer wired or wireless, they can also be connected to the network and converted into a central printer for use by all connected to the network.

The appearance of the printer had a tangible effect in everyday office life. Instead of spending weeks and months copying one book, for example, a printer can produce thousands of copies in a short time. There is hardly a company or organization that is free from the presence of a printer, even in the home, because of its availability at reasonable prices and various types.

Types of printers

The printers are divided into two types: the first is the Impact printer, and the second is the non-impact printer.

Collision printers

These printers work with the principle of the ways of the shape or letter to be printed via a tape of ink on the paper to print on it, and this type makes a loud noise and became very old, and among them are:

Daisy wheel printer

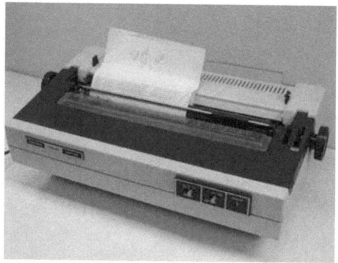

This printer is used to print letters, shapes and numbers, and it is not possible to print graphics as it contains a disk carrying letters, numbers and shapes. The ink ribbon in front of it is printed on the paper. This printer is similar to a typewriter, which is slow and no longer used these days.

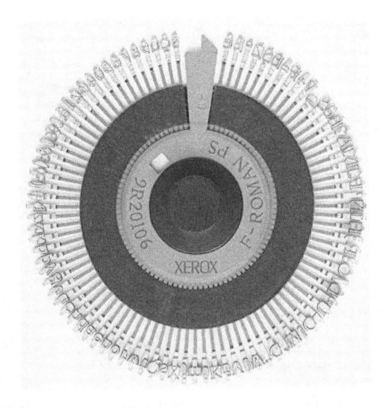

Dot matrix printer

This printer can print texts and graphics as it contains a print head consisting of 9 to 24 needles and moves on a left and right arm, and also contains hammers to push the needles at specific times toward the paper, which in turn hits the ink tape in front of it to print a point on the paper Thus, the shape or letter will print in its correct place. All the graphics or letters printed on the paper are made of dots, and the higher the number of needles, the higher the quality and accuracy of printing.

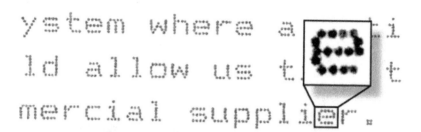

The image was published with the Creative Commons BY-SA license of Fourohfour.

The printing speed ranges from 100 to 600 characters per second, and printing can be done in basic colors only by replacing a color ink ribbon with black ink tape, provided that the printer supports this feature.

These printers were widely used in banks and institutions to print invoices and receipts that contain a second layer of carbon to print multiple copies simultaneously. This type of printer is inexpensive and outdated as it is no longer used due to the proliferation of inkjet printers.

Non-collision printers

Are printers that rely on a different mechanism for printing that is different from the principle of collision printers, so you find that this type of printers is less noise than collision printers, and their types are:

Ink-jet printers

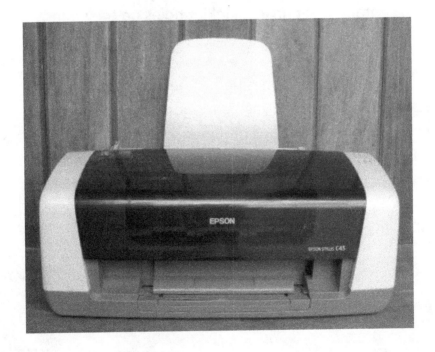

Inkjet printers stormed the world of printers in the sixties of the last century and spread rapidly because of the features it carries, such as its small size that suits homes and offices, and its printing accuracy of 600 dpi, its speed reaches 250 characters per second, and its sound Quiet while printing, and get cheap. All of the above features have caused users to switch from raster to this type.

This printer is similar in design to a dot matrix printer, and the most important parts that comprise it are:

Print head: It is the most important part of the printer and contains a set of small inkjet holes on the paper.

Ink tank: A small container inside which contains the necessary ink for printing. In monochrome printers (black color only) there is one container of black ink; the printers with color print have two containers, one for black ink and the other for color ink (Cyan, Magenta, and Yellow). There can also be a separate container for each color. Of the previous or more colors.

Paper tray: The place where the paper is to be printed.

Electric motors: Several motors are located inside the printer to move the printhead and ink containers back and forth to print on the paper, and to move the rollers that pull the paper from the paper holder towards the printhead.

Controlled circuits and memory: The printer contains electronic controlled circuits to receive information from the computer and then store it in random memory to translate it into a language the printer understands and then print.

When the print command is sent, the printer pulls a sheet of paper to prepare it, prepares and cleans the printhead to begin the process, and then moves back and forth stopping at specific places on the inkjet paper. Meanwhile, very small dots of ink size of micron multiples (up to 50 microns) emerge from very small holes in the printhead to settle on the paper very precisely, and if the printing is color, the colors mix together to form the desired color before reaching the paper. When finished, the head and containers return to their places after the cleaning process and clog the holes with a cap to prevent the ink from drying out.

There are two basic ways to inkjet from the print head holes:

Thermal Bubble Technology: It is used by many manufacturers such as Canon and Hewlett, and it relies on the principle of heating the ink through a resistance at the end of the hole when the print order arrives, which leads to evaporation and bubble formation, and its expansion leads to the ink coming out of the nozzle towards the paper and sticking to it . The number of nozzles ranges from 300 to 600 nozzles in each printhead from which the ink can come out at once.

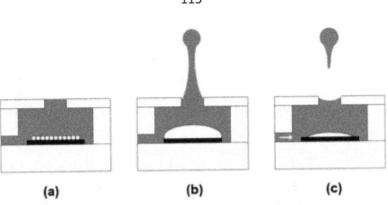

Image source: nanolithography.spiedigitallibrary.org.

Piezo vibrating crystal technology: Epson uses this technology and relies on the presence of a Piezo crystal placed at the end of the ink tank. The crystal vibrates when exposed to electrical charges. When the print order arrives, an electric charge is applied to that crystal, causing it to vibrate, the ink coming out of the nozzle, and sticking to the paper.

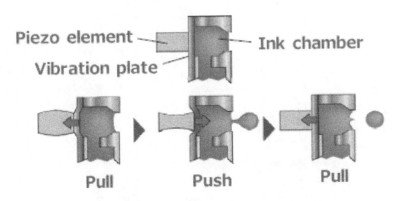

Image source: Epson.

Purchasing an inkjet printer depends on several things, the most important of which is the price. No one recommends purchasing an inexpensive inkjet printer, because the cheaper it costs, the more ink it costs. Sometimes you may pay more for the ink than the printer itself. It is also recommended that the ink containers be separate so that when one of the colors is out, you do not have to throw the container and buy a new one. Some containers are outside the printer, hoses are attached to the printhead, and can be refilled with ink again. So when you buy the printer, the focus is first on the ink containers and their price, then print speed, accuracy, and quality are second.

Laser Printers

It is one of the best types of printers, as it has a fast speed of up to 200 pages per minute per minute for large printers, print quality and high accuracy ranging from 600 to 1200 dpi with text and graphics. Xerox invented the first laser printer in 1971 and then began production of other companies, and was used exclusively in the field of office and then evolved and increased speed and quality with a lower price and thus spread more widely to enter the field of home use as well.

The laser printer consists of several parts, namely:

Control circuit: Contains all circuits, controllers, electronic elements and memory to receive data from the computer, store it in memory, and translate it into a language the printer understands. Among the most popular languages used in the conversion process are PostScript language, HP Printer Command language and OpenXPS language.

Drum-sensitive drum: The surface of this drum can be charged with static electric charges and affected by light, which modifies those charges.

Charging roller: It is located next to the light sensitive cylinder to charge its surface with negative electric charges.

Laser beam emitting device.

Mirror to reflect the laser beam toward the surface of the light-sensitive cylinder.

Toner cartridge: Toner contains toner, a powder of very small plastic particles mixed with black carbon or materials of other color and charged with a negative charge.

Paper holder: It is the place where the paperwork needed for printing is placed.

Wire to charge papers positively (available in expensive printers).

Cleaning blade, plastic blade to clean the surface of the photosensitive cylinder.

Fuser thermal heater for melting dry ink and securing it to the paper.

Roller rollers to pull and turn the sheets.

The printing process goes through several stages, as follows:

Image processing and preparing to print: When the print command is sent to the printer, the entire document or page is converted to a Bitmap bitmap in one of the description languages we mentioned and then stored in memory.

Charging process: In this process, any residual charges are removed from the previous printing process, then the surface of the photosensitive cylinder is charged via a cylinder or wire called Corona wire with negative charges as its surface can keep static electrical charges as long as it is away from light.

Writing process: In this process, the laser light is projected onto the mirror, which in turn reflects it on the surface of the light-sensitive cylinder in the places to be printed. Thus, negative charges are removed from those areas and remain without charge or shipped with an opposite charge and the image to be printed is formed on the surface of the cylinder. Meanwhile, the cylinder continues to rotate and the writing process continues.

Developing process: At this stage, the surface of the photosensitive drum is exposed to dry-charged dry ink, attracting it to areas that have been removed or reflected (the location of the image in the form of static charges). The density of the attracted ink varies with the power of the static charge. If the image is faded, the charge is low to attract a thin layer of ink particles and vice versa.

Transferring process: In the meantime, the paper comes after the image formation process on the surface of the light-sensitive cylinder for the ink particles to travel from the surface of the cylinder to its surface. Some printers have a positive charge pulley to enhance the gravitation and capture of ink particles.

Fusing process: The paper passes over a high temperature roller (200 ° C) that melts the ink particles and presses them to secure them well to the paper.

Cleaning: The surface of the drum then passes through a neutral charge plastic blade that removes the remaining ink particles, cleans the surface and prepares it for the printing process again.

These operations are consecutive and consecutive to complete the printing process. The color printing process of this printer is very complicated and sometimes suffers from errors in color. The color printer contains three containers of ink (Cyan, Magenta, and Yellow) in addition to black, as some printers use the "transfer belt" technology that passes in front of the three ink containers to transfer each layer of ink to it, and then the layers of the ink collectively move from it to the paper.

Other types of printers

We will review the following some types of printers that are designed for specific purposes:

Thermal printer

This printer adopts the principle of heating a paper that is very sensitive to heat in the places to be printed, which causes it to change its color and the appearance of the content as it does not need ink, and thus the image or letters are printed on the paper. They are widely used in printing receipts or invoices in banks, airports, transport stations, etc.

Source: Project IGM Group D.

Photo Printer

It is a type of inkjet printers designed for printing on photo paper with high accuracy, although it can also be used to print files and other documents. The printhead within this printer has a large number of inkjet nozzles, which increases the image quality.

Portable Printers

This type of printer is light in weight, small in size, and low in accuracy, although it is very expensive. Portable printers are either inkjet or thermal printers. Designed for users who travel a lot as it can be carried in a laptop bag, and can be attached directly to the camera or mobile phone.

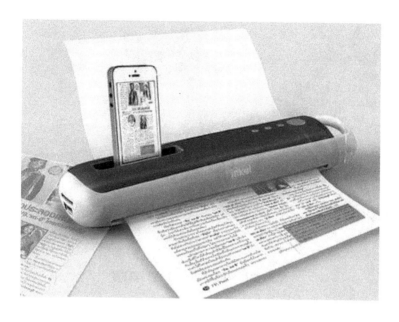

The multifunction printer

It is a multitasking device that mostly consists of a printer, scanner, fax and more.

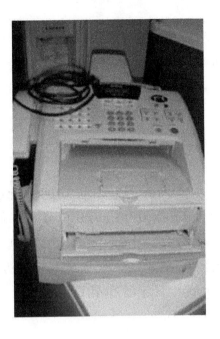

Chapter six

Introduction to computer networks: terms and understanding network layers

In this lesson, we will discuss the most basic basic concepts about computer networks; we will review the most important terms, learn about the mechanism of communication between devices by understanding network layers and review the commonly used protocols.

Terms

Before going into the networking world, you must start by defining some terms that you will find in your way as you expand in this field, whether in CompTIA A + certification or if you complete your path towards the world of networks. These terms and definitions are:

Network: A group of devices that communicate with each other in order to exchange and share files and information.

Communication: The set of operations and procedures necessary to transfer data between two devices connected over the network. Upon completion of the transfer process, the connection between them is lost.

Local Area Network: The abbreviation LAN refers to the phrase "Local Area Network", which is a small network located within a limited place or part of a non-large network, and an example of this network in the home or within the office or the company.

MAN: The abbreviation MAN refers to the "Metropolitan Area Network", which is the network that connects devices in one geographical area, it is larger than the local area network, such as the network that links the parts of the city together.

WAN: WAN stands for "Wide Area Network", which is the largest network of the two previous types, that is, it refers to large networks linking countries and continents, for example, the Internet.

Packets: The data is divided when it is transferred over the network into multiple parts according to its size, and these parts are called packets; that is, the units of information that are transported over the network. Each packet has a frame consisting of a header, a footer, and a body. Packet information such as the source address, destination, time, packet length, etc. are placed in the header and footer, and the data is placed in the body of the packet.

Network Interface: The network interface indicates hard network hardware. If one of the computers contains two network cards, each network can be controlled and set separately using the network interface.

Host: The computer connected to the network or the Internet.

Server: It is a computer that has high capabilities and features that works to manage the network and secure all services for hosts, and it works with a different operating system than regular operating systems such as Windows server 2012.

Peer to peer network: A network consisting of two or more computers that communicate with each other without a server. Each device in this network is responsible for itself, shares its resources with others, and uses their resources as well. Its protection level is low and it is inexpensive and can be created in the home, office or school so that the number of devices is not large.

Client / server network: A network containing a central server that manages and organizes the network between clients. This network provides a high level of protection and is more organized than the previous type and also more expensive and requires experienced people to manage it, and is used when there are a large number of devices connected to the network.

Protocol: A set of rules and processes that devices use to communicate and communicate with one another. There are a wide number of protocols such as TCP and HTTP which we will discuss later.

Port: A logical structure that refers to a specific process or service within a network where it is the last node in the communication process and completes the address of packets to direct to the desired site. Each port has a unique, non-recurring number indicating that service, and the port number is included in the packet information in the header.

Firewall: An application that has the powers to allow data to pass through or prevent it according to the rules and laws on which this application was built. The firewall also stops unused ports for protection from hackers and intruders.

These terms are not exhaustive, there are many of them that you will know as you expand in the field of networks.

Understanding how devices in the network communicate (network layers)

Networks contain different devices that are not similar to hardware or operating systems, and here comes to our minds the question: How do these devices communicate with each other over the network? The process of communicating and transmitting data over the network may be with the push of a button, but the processes that are performed to perform this are somewhat complicated, so in the meantime we will need to divide the network components and components into layers to understand this process.

OSI Model

This method was invented by the International Organization for Standardization in ISO in 1984 to explain how to network, and this model divides the OSI (Open Systems Interconnection) network operation into seven layers, namely:

Application: It is the closest layer to the user in which the user applications and users interact with each other. Examples of this layer are: e-mail, file transfer, telephony ... etc.

Presentation: This layer coordinates and prepares data for transmission over the network, and in this layer the data is compressed and encoded.

Session: This layer controls the communication process as it creates, manages and ends the connection between users.

Transport: It is the first layer that deals with the actual transfer of data, it represents a separation line from the previous layers that are closer to the user, and is responsible for establishing a secure and reliable connection, and ensuring the transfer and delivery of data without any error occurs and in the event of its occurrence, the data is re-sent, and is also responsible for Break big data into small pieces.

Network: This layer directs packets between different nodes in the network and chooses the best way to deliver data, and uses logical addresses (IP address) to indicate the source device address and destination.

The data is transmitted vertically through the layers, as each layer adds some information related to it as a header or footer. This process is called "encapsulation". Here the packets are formed for us, but the pieces and frames are similar to the packets but with different designations according to the layers. Examples of encapsulated information are: data format (video, text, etc.) in the display layer, and the logical IP address in the network layer.

When the receiver receives the data, the unwrapping process begins, which is the opposite of the previous process. It starts on each decoupling layer, read the header and footer information, and take the appropriate measures, then move to the top layer.

This process is similar to sending a message in the regular mail; Ahmed writes a letter and puts it in an envelope and writes in the letterhead the name and address and then sends it to the mail that encapsulates that message with a greater envelope and adds to it the address of the country or city or any information the mail operators understand to deliver the message to the recipient.

TCP / IP Model

Also known as the "Internet Protocol Suite", it was developed during the period of development of the OSI model and is simpler than it and spread widely until it became the primary way to communicate and connect to the Internet. The networking process in this model is divided into four layers, the function of which is similar to the OSI model:

Applications: Layers 5 through 7 are incorporated into the OSI model within this layer.

Transfer: similar to the transport layer in the OSI model and either provides good or reliable communications, depending on the type of protocol used.

Internet: deals with routing, route selection, and logical address addition (IP addresses).

Network access: deals with physical access to devices and media in addition to the way to access them and send data with the addition of physical addresses.

Protocols

The protocol has already been defined as the set of rules by which devices communicate with each other, and we will review some of the protocols used in the communication process.

Media Access Control

MAC is one of the communication protocols that are used to distinguish devices; each device is given an address by the manufacturer during its manufacture that distinguishes it from other devices while connected to the network.

This address remains fixed and cannot be changed even if the name of the device is changed via the operating system or any process, so this device can be specifically referred to, without the knowledge of its physical MAC address.

The physical address consists of a series of 48 bits and is divided into two parts; the first part is 24 bits and is given by the Institute of Electrical and Electronics Engineers IEEE to the manufacturer, meaning that each company is provided with a fixed address, and the second part 24 bits is provided by the device manufacturer and is responsible for it.

4A	AF	23	CC	A0	00
24 bit			24 bit		

IP is one of the most fundamental protocols for the functioning of the Internet, and is a unique logical address for all networks and devices connected to it. This address is provided in the Internet layer within the TCP / IP model.

With this address, it is possible to route data over the network in order to reach its destination and through it, determine the best way for the receiving device and choosing it.

An IP address consists of a string of 32 bits i.e. 0 and 1 divided into four bytes (each byte is eight bits) separated by a period and each byte is converted to decimal. An example of an IP address is "192.168.1.19".

Addresses are divided into categories (A, B, and C), where the class specifies the number of bits assigned to the network ID and the number of bits assigned to the host ID. Address Class A reserves the first eight bits of the network identifier and the first 0 bits are 0 in the first eight, and the second, third and fourth octets of the host identifier. This category is suitable for a small number of networks and a large number of hosts. Class B addresses are defined as having one and zero in the first two bits of the first eight; the first two bytes are reserved for the network and the last two bytes for the host. Class C starts with the first eight bits in series 110 and reserves the first three bytes for the network, and the last byte for the host.

The following table shows the value of the first octet that classifies network categories in decimal because the binary value cannot of course be memorized or remembered.

IP	The value of the first octet is in decimal form	The value of the first octet is in binary	The maximum number of hosts
A	1-126	00000001 to 01111110	16777214
B	128-191	10000000 to	65534

		10111111	
C	192-223	11000000 to 11011111	254

The previous IP address that we explained is for the fourth version IPv4 which is currently used, and because there are a large number of devices in the public network 32 bits are not enough, so the sixth version of IPv6 was developed which started to spread and use.

ICMP

ICMP stands for Internet Control Message Protocol. This protocol is used to send messages between devices to ensure they are available on the network or not connected. This protocol is used in network scanning and diagnostic programs such as the "ping" and "traceroute" command.

TCP

The Transmission Control Protocol is defined in the transport layer within the TCP / IP model, and can secure reliable connections. TCP encapsulates data in packets and transfers them across the lower layers, then ensuring that the data is received without error by waiting for a report from the recipient. This protocol is the most popular and widely used in the Internet.

UDP

The UDP (User Datagram Protocol) is similar to the TCP protocol and is defined within the transport layer as well; the difference between them is that the UDP protocol provides unreliable connections and does not make sure that data is delivered without errors to its destination, so this protocol is characterized by great transmission speed.

HTTP

The HTTP Hypertext Transfer Protocol is used in the application layer and is the basis for the web-based communication process as it transmits and exchanges text. This protocol uses port number 80.

FTP

File Transfer Protocol (FTP) is defined within the transport layer, and it transfers files from one host to another over the network. This protocol is unsafe so it is only used for general file downloads. This protocol uses port number 21.

DNS

The DNS (Domain Name System) is used in the application layer and converts host names into IP addresses. If you want to connect to a site, you only need to remember its IP address and just type the URL in your browser, such as academy.hsoub.com, and your device will search the DNS server in the network and ask it to convert the name to an IP address, then it uses the address it got in the process Connection. This protocol uses port number 53.

SSH

SSH (Secure Shell) is used in the application layer, which is an encrypted and secure protocol that can communicate with and control the remote server. This protocol uses port number 22.

There are many protocols that are not included in this lesson and they are of equal importance to the previous protocols, but that is enough to give you an overview of the basic techniques used in networks and the Internet.

Conclusion

After this lesson, it is assumed that you have surrounded some basic network terms, and got acquainted with the mechanism of communication between the various components together. This lesson will help you understand other lessons related to the networking field

Chapter Seven

Local network components

After getting acquainted with the method of communication between devices in the network in the previous lesson, we will complete in this lesson the topic of "network basics"; we will discuss the elements used in creating a local network and get to know its designs used.

You must know the network components and their functions in order to be able to create a local network that serves the purpose for which it was created. The usual components are: personal computers that represent network terminals, servers, and devices that provide network connectivity such as Hubs, Switches, and Routers;

we also have network cards and cables that are part of the local network.

Network card

In order for the computer to connect to the network, it must have a NIC (Network Interface Card); this card is placed within expansion slots or is often integrated with the motherboard and the network cable is connected to it, and each card has a unique MAC address.

The network card's job is to prepare data (data packets or frames) as they are sent or received, and to control the flow of data between the computer and the network. The network card operates within the physical layer of the OSI model that sends and receives data as bits over the network.

Distributor

The distributor is one of the simplest devices used to connect networks and is used in creating small networks. Computers arrive via cables to the distributor who works to receive the signal from one of the computers and then resends it to all its ports, i.e. the distributor receives data from one of the computers and then sends it to all connected computers; the destination computer accepts those data that carries its address while other computers neglect it.

This method is ineffective because the data is often sent to one computer, and the process of forwarding it to all computers causes a slowdown in the network, so the attention is turned towards the switch.

Switcher

The image was published with the Creative Commons BY-SA license of its owner, Geek2003.

The switcher is very similar to the distributed one, but it carries more advantages. The switcher does not send data to all computers, but can read the physical MAC address of the messages that reach it, then compare it with the addresses of computers connected to its ports and send it to its destination directly, so collisions decrease in the network and become faster, meaning that the distributor It works within the second layer of the OSI model.

The switch is frequently used in network construction and is more expensive than a hub, but it does a better job as it increases network speed.

the bridge

The work of a bridge is similar to a switch, but its job is to connect two networks together or split a large network into two parts to reduce collisions and increase its performance. When a device from the first network wants to communicate with a computer from the second network, the bridge allows that data to pass through it because it knows the MAC addresses of all computers connected to the network;

The router

The router connects the various local networks with each other and directs packets of data through them. If we want to connect the local network to the Internet, or we want to share the Internet with a group of computers or connect multiple networks with each other, we use the router.

Routers can distinguish the IP address of networks, computers, and packets sent, that is, they operate within the third layer in the OSI model, and store those addresses within a table called "routing table" with the indication of the road address or the next device that will lead to that network or computer. When the router receives the packets of data, it removes its packaging (see an entrance lesson to computer networks) and reads the address of the destination device and then compares it with the addresses in the routing table and chooses the best way to deliver the packets towards its destination and then repackages the package with the address of the switch or the next router and so the steps are repeated until Packets reach the switcher, which in turn sends them to their destination. The picture shows the process of sending data from one of the computers within the first network to a computer within the second network. The router chose the shortest path that passes through the second router with the presence of another road that passes through the third router.

Some routers also include a switch, so that it can be used to perform two functions at the same time.It can be dispensed with purchasing a separate switch and router; we use it if the network we want to create is for a small company or within the home; it may also integrate with the router a wireless access point, the choice of which depends on the nature of the place and speed And the cost.

Wireless access point

The wireless access point, called WAP for short, connects wireless devices such as mobile phones, laptops, or even desktop computers that contain a wireless network card to a wired network; similar to its altered work but without the presence of cables that connect devices, often connected to a router via Cable. They are widely used in hotels, airports, schools, companies, etc. Sometimes it is incorporated into the router.

Plug cables

Connection cables are an important component of the network that is used to connect different components. Data and signals are transmitted from one device to another in bits (0 and 1) as the cables operate within the first layer of the OSI model. There are three main types of cables, Coaxial cable, Twisted pair cable, and Optical fiber cable.

Coaxial cable

The image was released with a Creative Commons BY-SA license, to Apolkhanov.

The coaxial cable consists of an inner conductor surrounded by a tubular dielectric and then the insulation layer is followed by another conveyor surrounding it, and the cable is wrapped with a layer of plastic that may have an insulating layer with it. This cable transmits low-frequency electromagnetic signals; it is commonly used in television, radio, sound, and networks. It was used in the field of local networks as early as the eighties of the last century and it has two types: thick and thin until it is replaced by stranded cable.

Stranded cable

It is a cable consisting of four pairs of wires i.e. eight copper wires covered with an insulating material, all surrounded by an outer sheath. The purpose of the wire stranding in diodes is to reduce electromagnetic interference.

The first thing that was used for this cable in networks was a speed of 10 Mb / s, which is known as Class 3 (cat3 or category 3), followed by improved versions that differ from each other in the type of isolation and other things, including cat5, cat5e, and cat6 that have a speed of 100 Mb / s and even cat8.2 with a speed of 40 Gb / s.

There are two main types of stranded cable: Unshielded twisted-pair cable known as UTP, Shielded twisted-pair stranded cable known as STP; uninsulated stranded cable is widely used in Ethernet networks, landlines for cheap price of all types, its flexibility, And its good performance; As for the insulated stranded cable, it is characterized by the quality of signal transmission and the prevention of electromagnetic interference, and it has several types that differ in the way of isolation, as the insulation is only on the entire cable such as F / UTP, S / UTP and SF / UTP, or for each pair of wires such as U / FTP or both, such as F / FTP, S / FTP, and SF / FTP; the letter F indicates the word "Foil shiel." ding "is the insulating metal sheet, and the letter S to" Braided shielding "is the insulated stranded wire.

Stranded cables terminate with an RJ45 connector; RJ stands for "Registered Jack" for number 45 which indicates a specific model of link with eight carriers. The wires within the joint shall be installed in their specified locations and number from 1 to 8 starting from the left; there are two standards for the installation and arrangement of wires:

EIA / TIA T568A and EIA / TIA T568B; the following image shows these two standards.

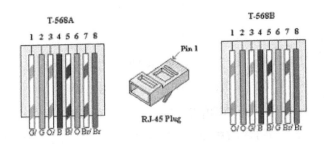

The existence of the previous two criteria makes us get two types of cables when configured:

Straight-through cables: The arrangement of wires at the ends of the cable is identical, that is, the arrangement of wires according to a single standard for both ends; they are usually used to connect different types of devices such as connecting a computer or server to switches or connecting a switch and a router.

Crossover cables: The arrangement of wires at the two ends of the cable is different, as the arrangement of the wires for one of the two ends of the cable is in accordance with the standard T568A and the other end according to the standard T568B; it is used to connect network elements of the same type such as the link between switches, routers, and even between computers, and servers between them.

Optical fiber cable

A cable that uses one or more optical fibers for transportation; this fiber is made of glass or plastic and is coated with an insulating plastic layer to protect it from interference. There are different types of it according to the desired purpose such as the transfer speed or the distance, the most important of which are: multi-mode fiber cable or single-mode fiber cable; the first is used for short distances and local networks, and the second for large distances.

Physical network diagrams

The process of linking network elements together is not random; there are several methods for creating a network and connecting its elements that define the network connection, the type of physical connection, and the characteristics of those connections. The scheme chosen relates to the number of devices and items available, and the required features of that network such as speed, performance, reliability, and cost.

Bus chart

In the serial pattern, the devices connect to a single cable, which is a coaxial cable. The cable transmits signals and data to all devices that the target device receives while other devices neglect it. Cable termination is important to prevent signals from returning and causing network errors from collisions. Any defective cable causes the network to go out of service.

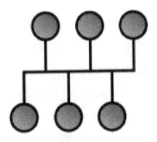

Star chart

In the astral chart there is a central device for connecting all devices as all signals and data transmitted through it pass; this device is in the usual local networks distributed, switched or directed; this scheme improves the network reliability because the failure of one of the connections will affect the device connected to that link only , And the rest of the network has nothing to do with that problem, but if the switch malfunctions, it will affect the entire network.

The network designed according to this scheme is easy to add new devices, and it is one of the most used networks.

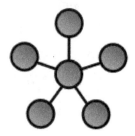

Ring chart

Each device in the loop connects to the device before and after it to form a loop; it may appear to resemble a serial chart but the devices are not connected to a single cable, and the cables are different here. The signals are transmitted from one device to another in one direction, which is retransmitted to the next device until it reaches its destination; an imbalance in one of these devices or cables will affect the entire loop, which represents a weak point, and to increase availability and reliability, the double annular scheme can be used, thus data can be transmitted in two directions.

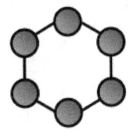

Full-Mesh

All devices communicate with each other in this scheme, which leads to high levels of error avoidance as there is no weakness that leads to network failure. Creating a network with this scheme costs a lot, and we note its use in WANs to connect branch offices and head office.

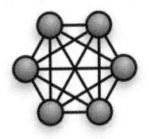

Sometimes due to exorbitant cost, we resort to other options that include a partial-mesh scheme, which is a compromise between ensuring that communication does not stop and the cost; in this scheme, the network branches or the most important devices are completely connected while the least important nodes are connected to another node only .

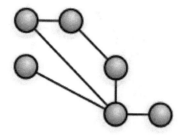

Conclusion

You now have a good introduction to networks that enables you to understand local networks such as how to communicate between devices, and know some of the protocols used, and the elements used to create them.

Chapter eight

Troubleshoot problems

After we got acquainted with all the elements of the computer with how they work, we will start in our lesson analyzing the faults of those for elements and knowing how to fix them; if you work in the field of computers or technical support then you must face the problems and malfunctions related to its elements then you are asked to search for the malfunction and the problem that led to stopping That component is out of business and repair.

In this lesson, we will discuss the most common malfunctions of three components: the motherboard, RAM, and the processor with a description of how to maintain them.

Motherboard problems and crashes

The motherboard is the main component of the computer that all other components are connected to so you will find that the possibility of malfunctions is great and this causes the computer to stop working, and this complicates the repair process and also makes it difficult to not be able to know the malfunction directly. There are always signs and signs that warn of the problem before it occurs, so if the user notices it, then the malfunction can be fixed before it becomes worse and if he does not notice it, this leads to a bigger problem and wider damage, and signs of the motherboard failure:

The peripheral devices attached to the motherboard are not recognized or displayed, such as the operating system does not recognize the hard disk or sound card.

Slow boot process indicates bad motherboard condition and may indicate malfunction of another item as well.

The computer does not recognize the devices that connect to the back ports.

Strange lines appear on the screen (if the display card is integrated with the motherboard).

The self-test process for the POST elements, ie computer and fans, does not start without anything on the screen (black screen only).

A fire smell or signs that an item is burning or discolored due to excess heat somewhere on the motherboard.

Old motherboard as some electronic components are restricted to a specific operating life, such as the failure of capacitors after a period of work.

A condensate swells or leaks its chemical.

The computer worked after several attempts to operate it.

Suddenly shutting down or restarting.

We should distinguish two phases when analyzing the motherboard malfunction: the first stage is the stage of passing the self-test process for the POST elements, and the second is that this process does not start or nothing appears on the screen.

In the first stage, if the computer skips the POST and enters the operating system and then the problem arises, other items such as the hard disk, memory, feeder, or cooling system ... etc. should be scanned. And make sure that they are intact; if the problem is not known, the motherboard must be checked.

The second stage is divided into two parts: the first is the appearance of the black screen with the work of the computer and the beeping sound from the speaker located inside the motherboard, in which case the motherboard is intact and the beep type must be distinguished to determine the malfunction; the beep sound indicates that the BIOS has started the testing process Self-POST sends signals to all elements to ensure their integrity and successive work such as starting to scan the processor, then the memory, then the display card, then the keyboard ... etc. Until you check all the hardware, if there is a problem with one of the devices, the process stops and an error code is sent and the amplifier beeps with a length and a specific number indicating the malfunction, such as a continuous and long beep sound indicating a malfunction in the memory, either it is not present or installed but does not work; it differs Error codes and beeps depending on the BIOS manufacturer.

The second section is the appearance of the black screen without hearing a beep sound; in this case we make sure that the amplifier is working, so it may not be present or not working; if it works and no sound is made, then the problem here is in the motherboard or BIOS; the BIOS problem is often solved by reprogramming it or Updating its content, while the motherboard must examine its electronic components (at least on the surface) and ensure that the feeder and processor and the northern bridge work; the method of examining the processor and the northern bridge or any integrated circuit is to operate the computer for a period of time, and suppose 5 minutes, then we turn it off and touch the surface of the processor after Remove the fan from it if it is hot or even A little warm it works, and we do the same thing with the north bridge and the remaining circuits; if the north bridge is cold and there is no heat in it then it is possible that one of his legs separated from the motherboard carriers because of the intense heat and to reconnect it we use the thermal station.

Before complicating things and our imagination going to a difficult hidden problem, we start with the simplest tests for the motherboard which are removing memory and operating the computer to make sure the beep sound appears, or we remove all elements from the motherboard such as memory, screen card and processor and we try to remove dust from them and then reinstall them, preferably using a spray that contains Liquid intended for cleaning electronic items, or we reset the BIOS to its default settings by removing the CMOS battery and connecting the carriers down with each other and pressing the power button for a few seconds; a high possibility that the problem will be solved and known as the performance of those things has solved with me a lot of problems and returned the The motherboard has to work to remove items, clean them, and then reinstall them while the user thinks there is a big problem.

Examination of the motherboard is very important to ensure that the fans are working or to search for an item whose color or shape has changed like it has burned or exploded, and also to ensure that there is no fire smell and look at all the elements in search of legs separated from the motherboard ostensibly.

On modern motherboards, the BIOS sends a clear message of the problem if the screen is working, such as showing a message that the CMOS battery is empty, or the keyboard or fan is not working or is not connected.

The more complicated the problem and the unresolved, the more certain that the cause is one of the electronic components, and then an expert in the field of electronics must be used to check the motherboard; most of the time the motherboards are not repaired in such a case, which forces us to buy a new one.

Sometimes we add a new item to the motherboard but it never appears as if you did not install anything or other problems occur by adding it such as the motherboard stops working or the black screen appears after its installation and the reason is that it is not recognized or incompatibility with the motherboard; this problem appears frequently as it becomes The motherboard is old and for its solution we can reprogram the BIOS (see motherboard lesson).

Crash test card

It is a card that is placed in one of the expansion slits and performs several tasks to troubleshoot problems such as measuring the efforts and frequencies of the motherboard and following the process POST to read and show the error code, and by searching for it in the manual of this card the problem can be found easily.

RAM problems and crashes

Memory malfunctions are minimal and are not uncommon in balancing with other elements because they do not contain mechanical parts. Symptoms of memory malfunctions are:

The blue screen or the death screen - as Windows users call it - suddenly appears and then the computer restarts; the blue screen may be a sign of a malfunction other than memory.

Restart the computer or the computer suddenly freezes.

The computer's performance decreases gradually after it starts, as the performance is good at first and then gradually decays.

The installation of a new application or operating system on the computer failed for an unknown reason.

Continuous or intermittent beep sound.

The computer worked with a black screen, and this sign is often preceded by the addition of new memory.

Two stages must be distinguished when dealing with memory problems; the first is that there is a problem with memory with the computer continuing to work and access to the operating system and this is represented in symptoms 1 to 4; in this case, it is not possible to say that the problem is in memory as it is possible that viruses or The operating system is the reason for that, so we examine the memory using memory scanning and analysis programs such as memtest86, memtest86 +, or Windows Memory Diagnostics provided by Microsoft on their systems. This program can be started by opening the "run" dialog via the shortcut "Ctrl + R" and typing "mdsched.exe" starts the memory scan process after restarting the computer, and then comes out D copies Aqlaaah of previous programs do not require an operating system.

The second case is the failure to complete the process POST and beeping or not beeping, and the reason is often the addition of a memory to the computer that does not correspond to the existing memory or is not recognized by the BIOS; in this case we make sure that the frequencies of the memories are compatible or change their position by placing both memories on Naughty expansion of the same color; the motherboard may not support this memory so we resort to updating the BIOS system. If the problem does not solve, we make sure the memory socket is working by reinstalling the memory on another socket or cleaning the memory buses and the socket with a spray to remove the dust, and this is a very common case.

A memory cell malfunction compels us to replace it, so we find that the only way to fix the memory is to replace it. In the event that the computer contains more than one memory, we remove them all and install one by one to check it; if all of them do not work then the socket may be the reason so we try the memory on another board to make sure that the malfunction is not from it and the socket malfunction is rare.

If the malfunction recurs at random, the probability that the problem will be in the cooling system or the feeder, but if the problem is repeated regularly then most likely that the malfunction is in memory; if you have an operating system and the problem appears in one of them without the other then the problem is not in the memory.

Processor problems and crashes

If the memory malfunctions are minimal, the processor malfunctions are almost rare, and if the processor is not working then there is no choice but to replace it.

A common problem with a processor is heat, in addition to malfunction or physical damage to the processor, such as when one of its legs is "broken" if it is of the type "PGA" due to being installed on the socket in a wrong way or falling while carrying it.

Overheating is the main reason that negatively affects the performance of the processor and reduces its life and stops suddenly if it exceeds the permissible limits. Symptoms of high temperature during work are restarting or the computer suddenly stops working; in this case the processor temperature should be monitored via Programs such as "CPU-Z" or by entering BIOS settings, Intel provides a tool to analyze its processor failures, a "Processor Diagnostic Tool" that provides many advantages to examine the processor, in addition to the availability of a bootable version for use if the system is not working.

The fan may be the reason for the high temperature such as low performance due to the accumulation of dust and dirt on it, or the failure of the cooling system as a whole efficiently or upgrade the processor or its speed without changing the fan or increasing its speed; some computer boxes provide holes for installing additional fans that can be used.

Some users believe that opening the lid of the computer box increases the efficiency of cooling, but this is wrong, as it disrupts the cooling system instead of increasing its efficiency.

In the event that the computer works with the appearance of the black screen and without a beep sound, we leave the computer running for a period of time and then turn it off and touch the surface of the processor to make sure there is heat; if there is no heat we try to try this processor on another plate to confirm its work or malfunction, and if that is the reason we replace It has a new processor.

Hard drive problems and crashes

The price of a hard disk may not be high compared to the motherboard or processor and its errors will not stop the computer from working except that its value to the user is as much as the value of the information in it. Some companies' hard drives contain valuable information and data that could pay millions to recover, if lost.

Since the hard disk contains moving parts such as motors, arm and disks, the possibility of malfunctions in it is possible. Some signs of hard disk damage and breakdown are:

Errors in reading and writing to and from the hard drive permanently or after the computer has been operating for a period or very slow while reading and writing.

The emergence of the blue screen (death screen) in the Windows operating system.

Slow start and entry to the system.

Files disappear.

No hard disk was detected during boot up.

Unusual loud noises from the hard drive when turning on the computer.

Hard smell from a hard disk, often after it is improperly connected or the feeder is damaged.

If symptoms 1 through 4 begin to appear, backup files should be taken directly, as the problem may worsen and fail to enter it again. It is highly likely that these symptoms are caused by viruses or errors in the operating system so before pointing the finger at the hard drive, you should make sure to Viruses or operating system have nothing to do with the problem. Defragmenting files often significantly speeds up the read and write process, so try this tool if the read and write speed is low or the system as a whole suffers from slowdowns and reduced performance.

If an error is found during reading and writing, such as the damage of a file that was working or no longer suddenly able to enter the operating system as a result of damage to one of the system files, the reason may be the damage and damage to some sectors; the reason for this is the sudden power failure from the computer or the computer moving during His work and his exposure to shocks, and all of this leads to scratching the reading and writing head of the disk surface to cause physical damage in the sectors in that location and thus destroying the data that is stored in it; God storage; prevent any system used to read and write, and this in turn leads to decrease the capacity of the hard disk. HDD regenerator is a good app for repairing bad sectors and has a boot version available.

There are many hard disk troubleshooting applications available, including:

Dell Hard Drive Diagnostics if your computer is from Dell.

Sea tools from Seagate.

Samsung HUTIL from Samsung.

Western Digital Data Lifeguard Diagnostic from Western Digital.

Most of these applications are available in boot versions. Windows has a built-in tool for finding hard disk and file system errors, and it can be run by typing "chkdsk / f" or "chkdsk / scan / r" on the command line.

The mechanical parts of the hard disk are made of metal and are known to expand with heat. You have to imagine what would happen if the hard disk heated and the arm extended, for example, parts of a millimeter ?! Reading and writing errors will occur and the problem will not go away until the temperature drops and the reading and writing heads return to their place, so the temperature of the hard disk must be monitored and preventive measures such as adding a fan or heat sink to the hard disk or improving the efficiency of the cooling system; the rate of occurrence of this problem in laptops more than Desktop computers.

In the event that the presence of the hard drive is not detected during the boot process, it must be verified that it is connected correctly. If the problem is not solved, changing the connections or the location of the port on the motherboard may solve it even though the failure of the port is rare.

Strange sounds from the hard disk caused by the failure of one of the mechanical parts after its fall or exposure to shock or due to a defect in the efforts connected to the hard disk Before installing a new one.

The process of recovering data from the hard disk when it is not working is the thing that most concerns the user; if the malfunction in the electronic circuit of the hard disk and the data is very important, you can consult a specialist in the field of electronics to try to fix it or you can buy a new hard disk of the same type and dismantle its electronic board and then install it Where the circuit breaks down; if the malfunction in the mechanical parts is inside the disk, it can be taken to a specialist who has the necessary equipment such as a vacuum chamber to disassemble it without damaging the disks, and it can recover data if the disks are delivered from physical damage.

Sometimes the feeder is the hidden reason behind the malfunctions of other elements, as all evidence may point to an element and when replaced it does not solve the problem and it becomes clear then that the feeder is the cause of this problem. There was a computer that made a continuous beep sound when it was running, which indicates that the memory was not working. After searching for the reason, it was found that the feeder does not provide the memory with the effort required to operate it, and therefore the safety of the feeder must be checked before anything.

The feeder has limited capacity and overflow causes it to stop working; adding new items or replacing newer items with old items may increase the pulled capacity of the feeder and malfunction.

The feeder may be partially malfunctioned, such as some efforts being stopped or not working, and this causes some elements to stop working.

Conclusion

In these two articles, we learned about many faults of the basic elements of the computer with how to solve them; the topic of troubleshooting is gained by practice and practical experience and is not limited to the most common previously mentioned faults but its scope is broader than that, and we must also focus on the way to deal with the problem and give it some attention because it is the way To reach a solution.

CPSIA information can be obtained
at www.ICGtesting.com
Printed in the USA
FSHW011013131120
75906FS